NAKED *before* God

Words that express my heart

BY WILLIAM OWENS

Copyright © 2015 by William Owens, Jr.
All Illustrations in this book are the sole property of William Owens, Jr.
Cover Illustration and all inside illustrations by Luisa Rachbauer
Inside layout by WorldTech
Editing by Barbara Williamson Cook

All rights reserved. Any resemblance of illustrations to actual persons, living or dead, or actual events is purely coincidental. No part of this publication may be reproduced, distributed, or transmitted in any form or by any means, including photocopying, recording, or other electronic or mechanical methods, without the prior written permission of the publisher, except in the case of brief quotations embodied in critical reviews and certain other noncommercial uses permitted by copyright law. For permission requests, write to the publisher, addressed "Attention: Permissions Coordinator," at the address below.

Printed in the United States of America
First Printing, 2015
978-0-9824027-8-8

Published by
Through People.com

For booking information contact:
www.nakedbeforeGod.com
william@nakedbeforeGod.com

TABLE OF CONTENTS

INTRODUCTION	1
NAKED BEFORE GOD	4
WORDS	6
HARD I FOLLOW	8
THE HEART OF MAN IS IN YOUR HAND	10
I TRUST YOUR LOVE	12
O MY STRENGTH	16
I HAVE TO LET YOU	18
UNLESS YOU	20
YOU CAN AND YOU WILL	22
IF YOU WANT IT	24
NOTHING ELSE	26
IN HIM	28
COMMUNION	30
MY MIND RACES	32
WHAT MORE CAN I GIVE	34
I PONDER	36
I STAND ALONE	38
TEMPER ME	40
BE KEPT	42

JOLT MY MIND	44
INWARD MAN RENEWED	46
CONTEMPLATE TO CALCULATE	48
LET ME NOT	50
WHO I SEE IS NOT ME	52
NOT WHAT I FEEL	56
DOESN'T MATTER	58
THE DARK LIGHT OF MY SOUL	62
I JUDGE MYSELF NO MORE	66
ALL THAT MATTERS	70
SHADES OF LIFE	72
I SEE THE PAIN	74
SCARS	78
WHY?	82
MY MOTHER	86
DANGEROUS WONDERS	88
SLANDERED	90
THE ENEMY WANTS YOU TO SEE	92
I AM A SPIRIT	94
SPIRITUAL RHYTHM	96
HEART CORDS	98

THE TRUTH DOES NOT SCARE	100
TO LIVE IS TO FORGIVE	102
I TURN	104

INTRODUCTION

Poetry?

I never set out to write poems, nor did I read poetry.

"Words that express my heart" represents my time with God. My poetry is the result of the difficult and lonely season in my life. During this period I had to choose to either react or respond. Not only did I choose the latter, I also decided to peel the mask off one layer at a time and get "naked before God."

I literally bare my inner thoughts, unclothe my issues, uncover my fears, unmask my ideas and unveil my hopes. I even unshroud my sins -- especially my sins. Bare in mind it's the little sins that are hidden and covers us and really holds us down.

Getting naked is difficult enough -- even when no one is watching. Getting naked before God is much more difficult when God allows us to permit Him to see your heart open and expose yourself as you willfully uncloak yourself.

Becoming naked before God is no doubt difficult both emotionally and mentally because by our very nature, we can't tell what it really means to be naked -- let alone being naked before God. I mean, how do you know if you are baring your soul before the one and true Living God and not some made up entity that's nothing more than a figment of your imagination? I believe that answer is found in what happens when you begin to remove the mask. It is when God in turns opens His heart to you.

In every way, these poems are God's heart being open to me. It does not necessarily mean the answer is crystal clear. It just means that somehow it works. You will notice my moment of getting naked in the beginning of "words that express my heart." It is then towards the end you will read a response or answer – that's God speaking back to my heart. That's how I know I got naked before God!

It is critically important to point out that God never speaks contrary to His Word – The Holy Bible – nor does He speak through any other than His Son – Jesus Christ or the Holy Spirit.

Most of these poems are personal. While other poems are observations of people who have come into my life. Some of these people I know well. While other individuals are strangers. These poems represent moments in time which I was captured by their experience and the words were liberated.

I do not follow the prescribed or standard poetry protocol. I would not recognize it if I was even looking at it. Remember? This is about me being naked before God.

Everyone has a naked place that is never safe when opened to strangers. You simply never know what their reaction will be. I can only hope that these "words that express my heart" will add a source of courage and hope to your life and help you to start unclothing yourself and get NAKED…. Before God!

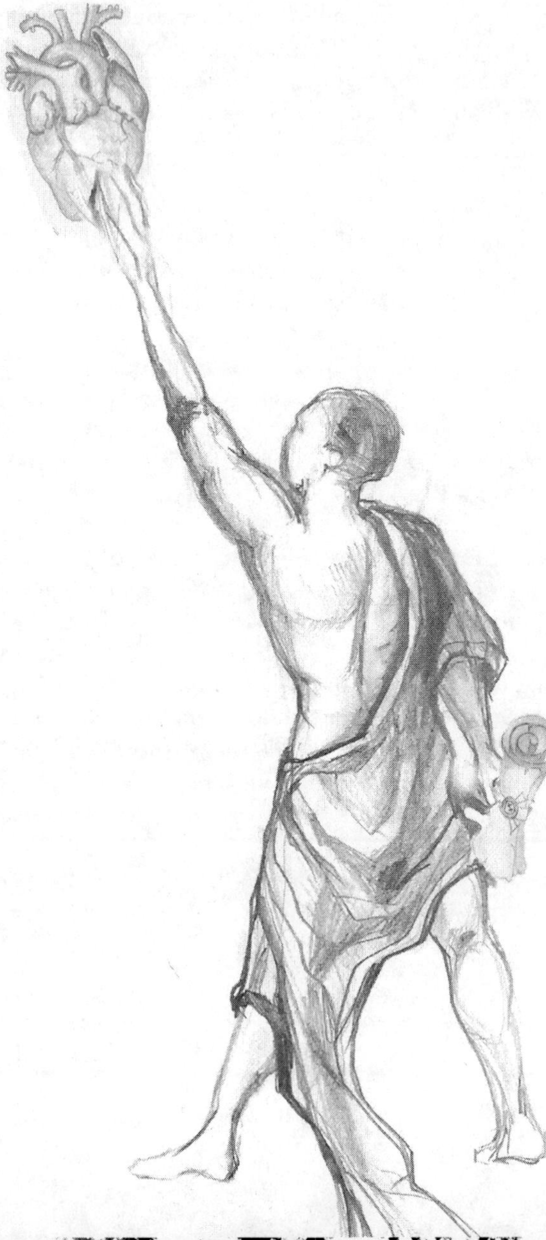

NAKED BEFORE GOD

The birth of words
Burst forth from the womb of my heart,
Sowed by seeds from time spent with God.
Expressions of my inward man;
My mind,
Emotion,
Sole devotion
To Him.
For Him,
By Him,
In Him
Do I live.

The birth of Words;
Painful contractions
Of conflict,
Rejection,
Ostracized.
Causes reflection
Upon Him.
Now drawn near
To me with words,
Burst forth from the womb of my heart.

No lack of birth,
No slowness of flow.
Stay near Him.
The words break forth
Ever giving birth to the inward
expressions of my heart
as I lay bare,
Naked Before God!

Enjoy the video commentary and reading of this poem by William Owens

WORDS

Words,
We think
We create.

But we are the vessels, by which they procreate
In our minds, unveiled to be captured within the
Vortex of time.

To collide with expressions of the spirit world, regardless Of the
rhyme or rhythm that might come forth.

Though we, through pride do think we speak truth,
Our fears reveal our doubt.
Manifested through word drought, attest by soul drop
Voice pitch as we attempt to avoid that ditch.

The ditch
In which our souls be found,
We play it dumb
Less we be exposed and be found
out...

To be a word bearer void of the essence of the words we speak,
But desperate to find hope in them.
Naked we stand,
Hoping to dress ourselves with words belched
from hollow souls,
desirous to be clothed upon with truth.

Yet refusing to let go of the contradiction of
Condemnation we feel,

In hopes that words will bring redemption that we seek.

Words,
We think,
We create
But we are the vessels by which they procreate.
He is the Word manifest,
To attest
Authority over all Words.

Words that give life,
Expose death,
Resurrects,
Perfects,
Utters a new dialect.

Words,
Not our own,
Reveal our fears,
Our hopes,
Our dreams.

Words are His.
Words are Him.

HARD I FOLLOW

Based on Psalms 63

My soul presses pass distractions
Before my eyes,
Prepares for my mind to rise

To dig my heals in ground beneath,
To follow hard after Him who
Captured me,
Died for me,
Redeemed me.

No hand but His
Sustains,
Upholds,
Makes hold,
Satisfies,
The hidden man of my soul.

Early do I rise without vanities
Running through my mind.
Knowing He only satisfies
My bleeding heart inside.

Unashamed I testify
Thou art my God.
Early will I seek Thee
To thee alone will I arise.
Will I cry,
Will I plead
For thy right hand to
Be upon me?

No life have I without Thee.

Listen all flesh...!
Inhabitants of land apostate,
I bless Him.
I lift my hands to Him.
My lips alone give Him
PRAISE!

....

Enjoy the video
commentary
and reading of
this poem by
William Owens

THE HEART OF MAN IS IN YOUR HAND

The heart of man is in your hands,
You turn it to fulfill
Your pleasure
Your purpose,
Your plan.

His mind is yours,
wired in perfect symmetry
to perform,
to pursue,
to plow towards
the destiny
set in their hearts
before time begun.

I TRUST YOUR LOVE

I trust your love;
Gripping me deeply,
Exposing me gently,
Healing me completely,
From the nix of life that happen.

Callused.
Cold.
Confused.
Can't
Connect.

Down.
Dragging.
Deranged.
Deformed.
Discontent.

I trust your love;
Gripping me deeply,
Exposing me gently,
Healing me completely,
From the nix of life that happen.

Bothered.
Bruised.
Bullied.
Baited.
Busted.

Tainted.
Tarnished.

Ticked.
Talked about.
Thrusted.

I trust your love;
Gripping me deeply,
Exposing me gently,
Healing me completely,
From the nix of life that happen.

Returned.
Redeemed.
Revived.
Reconciled.
Reborn.

Alive.
Always
Abounding
Abba.
Atoned.

I seek to feel
As if that is real.
To find a touch,
A hug,
A kiss.
Thinking the flesh of others
Will somehow heal.

Thinking their mind
Can grasp
The complexities
Of me.
Deep seeded
Animosities

That fester,
That froth,
That attract broken people
Not capable of offering hope.

I see in them what's in me,
Inviting misery.
No healing,
No joy,
No zeal.
Nothing restored.

Foolish.
Fake.
Fussing.
Flat.
Frowning.

Though I want what I see,
Instead I choose to trust in thee.
You know what is best.
You know what is good.
You know what is perfect for me.

Standing.
Singing.
Soaring.
Surrendered.
Shouting!

- That -

I trust your love;
Gripping me deeply,
Exposing me gently,

Healing me completely,
From the nix of life that happen.

If it be possible take this cup from me.
Nonetheless not what I will,
But your will be done.

I trust your love.

....

Enjoy the video
commentary
and reading of
this poem by
William Owens

O MY STRENGTH

Based on Psalms 59

Men judge me,
Choose not to know me.
Eyes avoid me,
Scatter away from me.

It's not me,
Its not them,
It's Him!
Unto Thee O my strength will I sing.

Despised I might be,
Judged by the empty righteousness of mortal man.
Blinded by reason learned from another,
Maybe his mother.

Compacted by fears of his own,
Afraid to stand alone.
Not able to see truth revealed,
Eyes sealed,
Thinking he's real.

It's not me,
Its not them,
It's Him!
Unto Thee O my strength will I sing.

God is my defense.
God is my king.
Out loud to Him
O my strength will I sing!

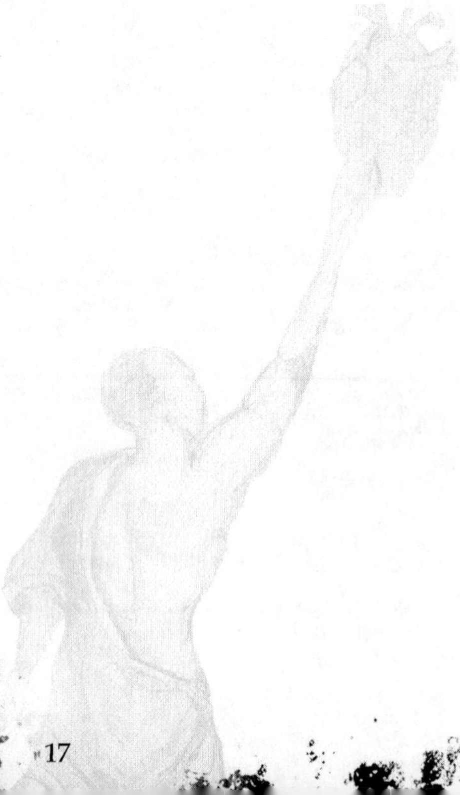

I HAVE TO LET YOU

I have to let you do what I can't do.
Let you show me what I can't see.
Yield to you to be what I can't be.
Trust you,
Not trust me.

I have to let you show me how to love me.
Show me how to love others unconditionally.
It's You in me that my life can be.
You in me that I truly become
The person I'm searching to find.
To discover,
To celebrate
The me I am,
And there is no other.

I have to let you do what I can't do.
Let you show me what I can't see.
Yield to you to be what I can't be.
Trust you,
Not trust me.

....

Enjoy the video commentary and reading of this poem by William Owens

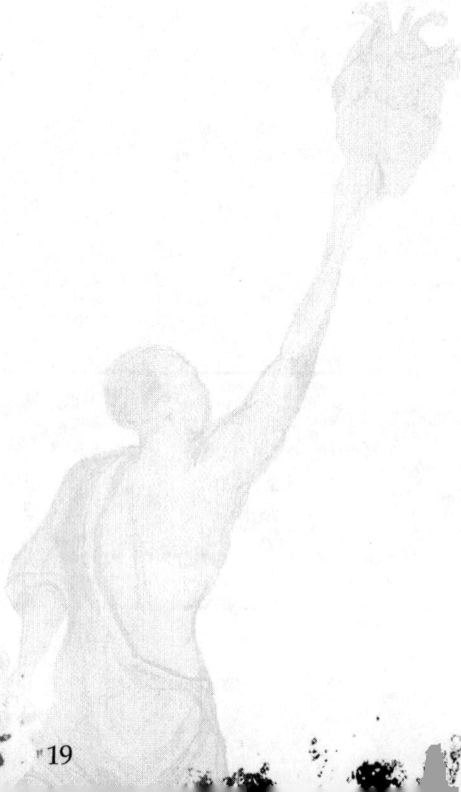

UNLESS YOU

My labor is nothing unless You are there.
My ideas are vain unless You spoke them in my ear.

My cares, the things I dread, my fears, worry, tossing and turning in my bed.
All do nothing unless You are there.
I'm dead, done, always on the run.

Unless You are You I can never be
Unless You are near I'll never be free
Unless I draw near to You, why would You draw near to me?

Unless means yes
If I seek You with all my hearts best.
Unless is profound if I submit and come around.
Unless is a test of my will's resolve.
Unless is safe, if it reveals just where You are.
Where I can be,
How I can live,
Why I can see

Unless
You....

There is no
Me....

Yes -
You
Do.

Enjoy the video commentary and reading of this poem by William Owens

YOU CAN AND YOU WILL

You can and you will
If I yield and be still.

You did and you do
Uninhibited by yesterdays.
Contrary experiences fresh in my mind.

You were there and you are here,
To dissolve the pain and redeem the time.

Power unknown.
Reach uninhibited.
Voice profound.
Cross extended.
Impacting my mind.
Unraveling my wound.
Restoring my soul.
Removing the bruise.

You can and you will
If I yield and be still.

....

Enjoy the video commentary and reading of this poem by William Owens

IF YOU WANT IT

If you want it let it be,
If not; be it far from me.

If of you let it live.
If of me let it die.

If of you - I will gasp.
If of me - I will sigh.

Of you,
By you,
Through you,
For you.

I live.

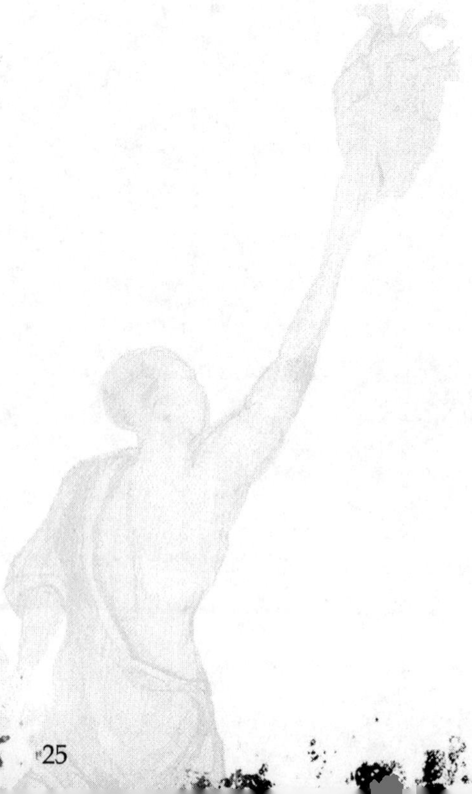

NOTHING ELSE

There is nothing else to do
Than to find my place in you.
Nowhere to be
Than to draw near to thee.

My place with you
Sets my day.
Drawing near to you
I hear you say
Your will within my core.

Vision imparted,
Faith ignite
Spirit rises
Prepared to fight.

For therein do I live
Where revelations flow.
Where divine insights are given,
Mysteries that my enemies do not know.

There is nothing else to do
Than to discover time and time again;
Day by day that comes
My place,
My life,
My being
In you.

Enjoy the video commentary and reading of this poem by William Owens

IN HIM

We inhibit Him,
We limit Him,
We through fear deny Him.

We judge Him,
Run from Him,
Always afraid to come to Him.

We accuse,
We malign ,
We reject out of our minds
HIM.

The maker of everything,
Creator of our souls.
Provider of our breath,
Our food and our clothes.

Lover above all lovers,
Tender beyond compare.
Never leaving or forsaking us
Promised to always be there.

Say no evil against Him,
Submit yourself to Him.
Embrace the power from Him,
Be changed,
Be Rearranged.

Inhibit Him no more,
Put limits out the door.
Run toward Him,

No longer fear Him.

You bless Him,
You worship Him,
You dance,
You rejoice,
You sing.

In Him you live,
In Him you move .
It's now in Him
You have your being

COMMUNION

Communion
Creates a union.
God with me,
Me with God.
Blissful infusion.

I find my place.
I settle my mind.
I remove the distractions
of every kind.

I take hold of soul.
Release my spirit
Take flight toward heaven.
Not far
Within.

Sense His presence,
Hear His voice.
Joy imparted,
No place for sin.

Heart connected,
Peace received,
Will revealed,
Mind at peace.

Communion
Creates union.
God with me,
Me with God.
Blissful infusion.

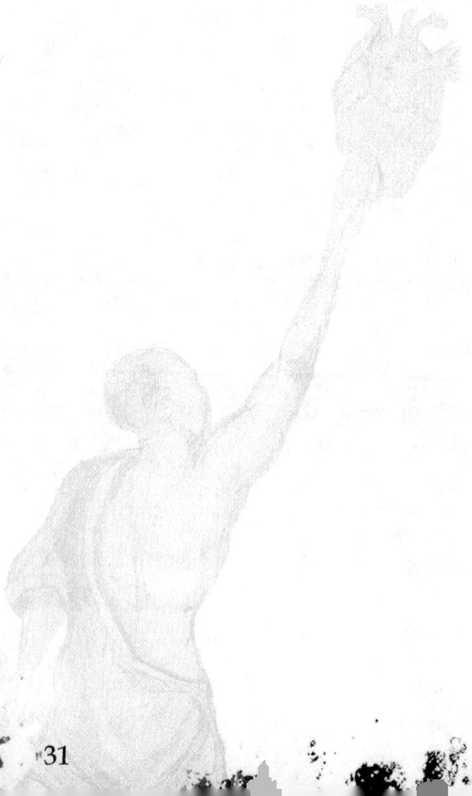

MY MIND RACES

My mind races to places,
Looking for traces of evidence
Of my purpose.

My lungs breathing heavy
Exhausted at the exercise of seeking.
The trouble of searching,
The vexation of ever learning,
Yet left without knowing.

My mind races to places,
Looking for traces of evidence
Of my purpose.

Occupied activity,
Not necessarily for me;
Petrified of doing nothing.
Insecure,
Fractured,
Running into something
To be fulfilled.

Picking work
Like flowers in a field,
Thinking the work will make me healed.
Activity of any kind
Yet bored out of my mind.

Because -
I know in my being
There is more.

Hear it in the deepest crevice of my very essence,
Yet to know is not enough.

Where,
Who,
How?
When
Will this misery end?

What must die in me,
That I may live to know
The calling I hear
Inside my soul?

Who will set me free
From the sentence of drudgery,
That gets ugly the more I do me?
WHO is HE?

Able to stop the race of your mind,
Provide the evidence.
Make known your purpose,
Satisfy your deepest thirst every time.

It is Jesus
Whose mind understands.
He too was a man
Tempted yet without sin.

Your mind at peace
Your race brand new.
Rest,
Reset,
Begin afresh.

WHAT MORE CAN I GIVE

What of me doeth hath value?
What of me can bring forth?
None of me equals matter,
Such is reason I need you more.

Vain and filth compass my soul.
Darkness and despair await me there.
No hope found within myself,
But Jesus - my Savior alone redeems.

To him I owe all my essence.
Through Him
I've been born again.

Now I live a life of freedom.
Now through Him I bring forth fruit.
All of me equals victory,
Such is reason I abide in Him.

Onward as a warrior fearless.
With sword drawn and shield raised, Fight this battle as His
faithful servant.
Fulfill the call until the end of days.
What more can I give?

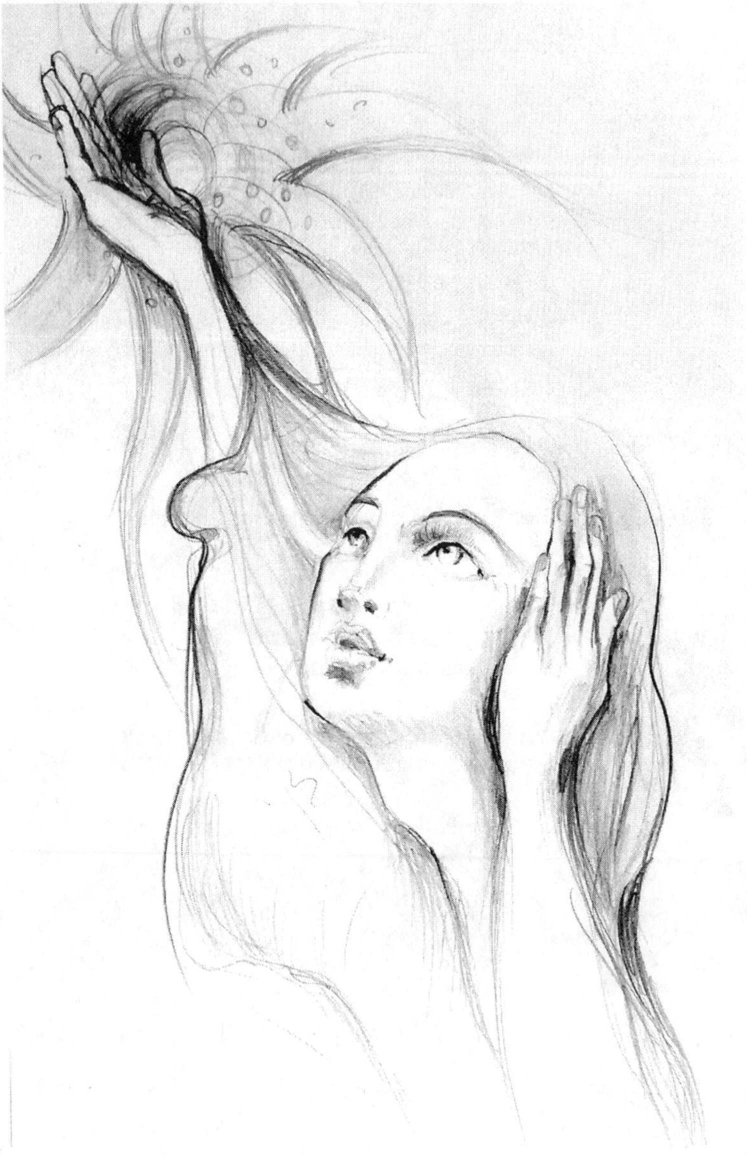

I PONDER

With hand on face I ponder my place.
Within my mind
Upon my heart.
Around the souls where I breathe, where my eyes do see
My ears do hear
It is my space.

Beneath the stars that gaze on me
I wonder who they see me to be.
The Sun that shines,
The clouds that cruise,
The moon - so cool
They know their place.

Fear visits me.
Telling me
To see Things I must agree to see.
Strange they exist in my mind
But not before me.

Faith arises in my soul,
It is here that I feel bold.
To stroll within my spirit to mountain tops.
Skies of eagles
Races unfathomable.

I seize upon a glimpse of my place within this realm of faith,
Not found within my mind.
Upon my heart
Amongst others,
Or even in the stars.

Found with my hands off my face,
Instead they are up and raised.
Raised to the Creator by whom I'm made
Who I embrace and am embraced by faith.

Who became me to understand me;
To be touched by the feelings of my infirmities.
To reconcile my life a solved mystery,
Known by him before the world knew itself.
Loved by Him today,
Secure with Him forever.

I do rise,
Break free,
Celebrate.
Run my race by faith
Hand off my face.
They are up and raised,
I have found my place
In Him
I LIVE,
I move,
I have my being.

....

Enjoy the video commentary and reading of this poem by William Owens

I STAND ALONE

I stand alone in my room,
Reaching,
Stretching,
Lifting my hands to you.
Desperate to be graced upon
By your tenderness.
To be favored,
To be blessed.

I stand alone in my room
Facing the flood of vanities
Staring at me.
Burning in me, holding me in captivity.
To extract passions hidden deep within my souls cavity

I set myself,
I confine myself,
I arrest myself to be disposed to thee alone.
To take hold of thy throne
'Til your hold has gripped my soul.

I stand alone in my room
'Til your presence has engulfed me.

....

Enjoy the video
commentary
and reading of
this poem by
William Owens

39

TEMPER ME

Temper my body, my mind, my eye.
You are my God, my prize, my life.

Wisdom bestow upon,
Patience arise within.
Joy of my Lord strengthen.
All this be to me
As I humbly yield to thee.

Arrest the lust that doeth arise.
No reason, no rhyme,
Just shows up with ideas
From time to time.
I do cast down
To the ground
This clown,
Who seeks to manifest this flesh
To undo the rest I've found in you.
With authority invested in me I resist
I stay free.

Temper my body my mind, my eye;
You are my God, my prize, my life.

Spirit Life m
Real beyond the real I see.
Spirit to my spirit,
You are to me
Truth unveiled intimately.
Your voice I hear inside.
This life I live,

This life I am.
Tempered
Patient,
Wise.

Temper my body, my mind, my eye.
You are my God, my prize, my life.

BE KEPT

When I want to be kept, you keep me.
If I want to be free, you free me.
As I yield to thee I live,
When I yield to me death takes hold.
Life erodes.
Dead end roads.

Come back to you immediately.
Restore my being,
Break forth in song.
Freed I am
No work performed.

Be kept,
I yield, I yield
To thee.

43

JOLT MY MIND

Jolt my mind to clear it from ideas created by me.
Jolt my mind to create clarity that I might see.
Jolt my mind from ideas that keep me from being free.
Jolt my mind from time to time,
That my life would be aligned.
With heavens will,
With the coming kingdom.
With perpetual freedom,
Jolt my mind.

INWARD MAN RENEWED

Based on 2 Corinthians 4:16-18

Why are you living for the man that's dying?
Everyday smells of decay.
Don't have a clue,
Can't do,
Undo
Always undone.
On the run from shadows
Clawing,
Snarling,
Spitting,
Always tripping.

Start living for the man inside.
Renewed daily to fly,
To soar above the sky.
A glory not known through
Intellect that dissects.

The man inside looks not with eyes in head on the temporary state,
He sees with eyes of spirit.
Eternity.
Things not seen.
Things revealed does he originate and orientate his being.

Eternity is the weight
By which he weighs his life.
Renewing that inward man
Assures the prize.

Looking not on things seen,
This man through eternities gaze sees everything
As it really is.

....

Enjoy the video
commentary
and reading of
this poem by
William Owens

CONTEMPLATE TO CALCULATE

Contemplate to calculate
Only to facilitate.
Contradictions confronting
The truth of who I am;
Of what I want,
Of who I love,
Of why I want it
That I am loved.

Contemplate to calculate
Only to facilitate.
Contradictions confronting
Hidden motives deep within.
Revealed by small words,
Subtle deeds,
Tiny slashes that doeth bleed.

Contemplate to calculate
Only to facilitate.
Contradictions confronting
People who think they know me.
People who I think I know,
Rid ourselves of this foolishness
That deceives both our souls.

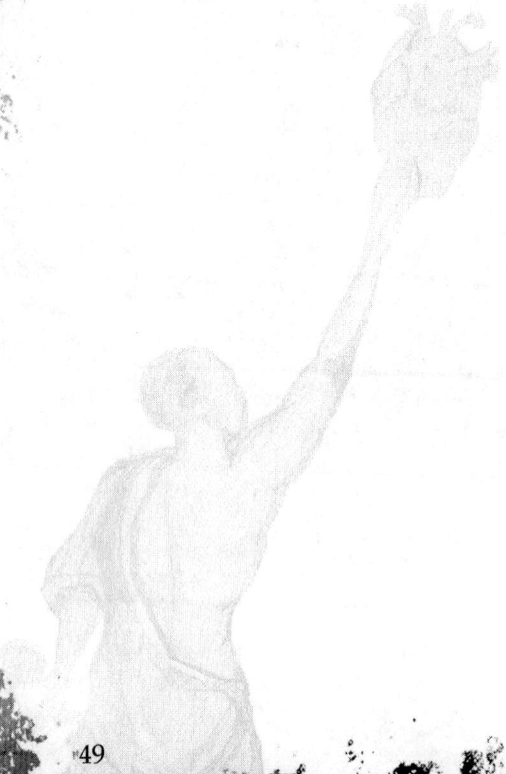

LET ME NOT

Let me not be deceived by me,
Let me not lie to justify
Reasons why I live.

Courage - arise in my mind
Take hold of purpose before me.
Refuse to entertain ideas that seek to rearrange your will
revealed within my being.
Born before the start of time

Let me not be deceived by me.
Let me not lie to justify
Reasons why I live.

Souls who seek to feast on me
Show me who they be.
My own lust blinds me,
Therefore I choose to see what I want to see.

Lest I see You I don't see me,
I am blind.
I become prey to such souls,
My worst enemy to my mind.

Let me not be deceived by me,
Let me not lie to justify
Reasons why I live.

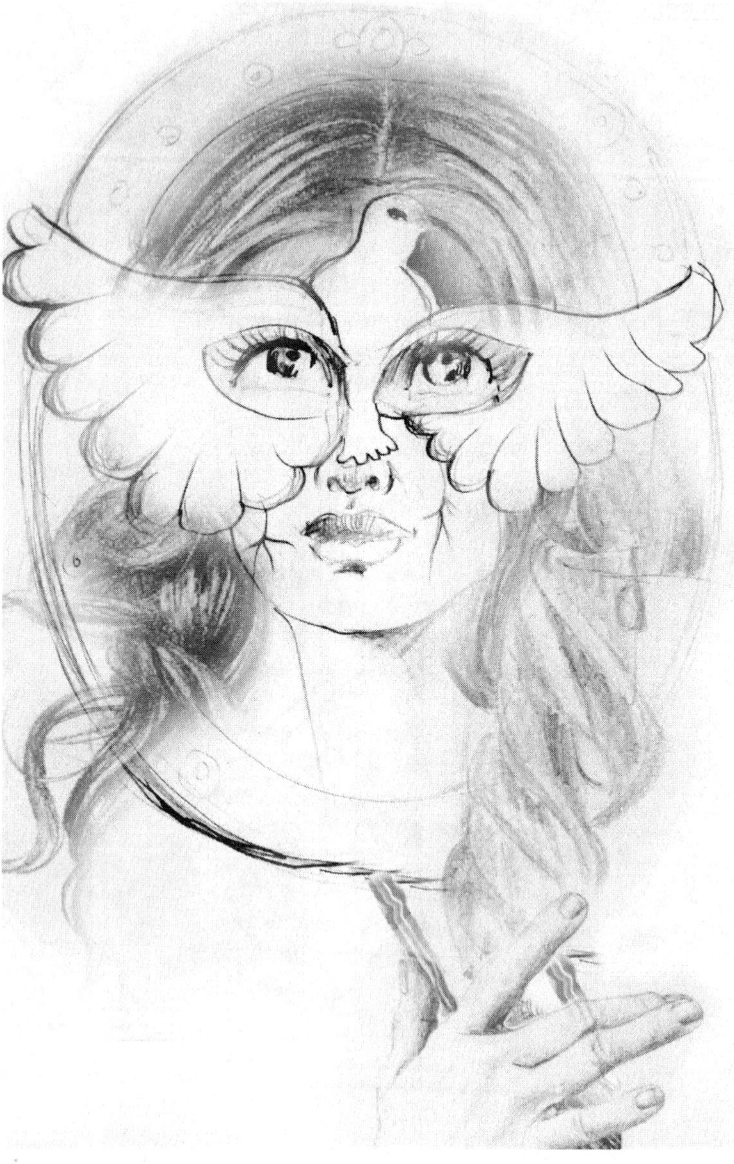

WHO I SEE IS NOT ME

Who I see is not me.
Who I feel is not real.
What I think is born of a temporal idea, false illusions,
Assumed conclusions.

Who I perceive myself to be
Are fault lines - hidden to me.
Others who attempt to arrange my fate, direct my face,
Determine my place in this universal complex that knows no space

Deeper and deeper still I know I'm real.
Testing all manner of creation,
Tasting every flavor of religion.
I, like a pigeon, fly to every rooftop looking for affirmation of my existence.
Validation of my creation.
My wings are tired.

I look within,
Only to find more reasons why
That won't fly.
Unless of course I manipulate what's not there... and just lie.
Lie to myself and therefore to others.
Don't risk the shame.
Convince,
Persuade,
Get swept up in this parade.

I must break away,
Tear off this mask.
There must be more

I dare to ask... God.

GOD;
WHO AM I?
You are mine
Made before time.
Made with me intertwined in all of you.
Made to feel after me,
Search after me,
Draw near to me,
Be one with me.

I'm not a god made by you.
I'm The Only God who created you.
Intelligence,
Emotions,
Self Will
Makes you unique.
Makes you like Me, but not Me.
In need of Me to be who you really are.

There is One way to me,
None other.
A Redeemer who can destroy
The stain that strains your heart,
The poison that convicts your mind,
The guilt that assaults you time after time.

A Redeemer
To represent you before me;
To give you a mind heart and spirit that's guilt free.
This will prove that I Am.
Will reveal that you are mine,
Not who you see yourself to be.

That redeemer is Me,
Revealed through my Son.
You know. .. He's the only one.
The only way,
The only Life
He's Jesus - the Risen Christ.

....

Enjoy the video
commentary
and reading of
this poem by
William Owens

55

NOT WHAT I FEEL

It's not what I feel
That speaks of what is real.
It's not what I see
That is there.
Not what I hear is truth
Not I but you.

Matters little
What man believes;
confusion of face
when reading the leaves.

Searching all creation
For an explanation
Of what is,
Of who I am,
Of where I go,
Of where I be,
Orientation eludes me.

It's not what I feel
That speaks of what is real.
It's not what I see
That is there.
Not what I hear is truth
Not I but you.

Enjoy the video commentary and reading of this poem by William Owens

57

DOESN'T MATTER

Doesn't matter how much I see myself to be;
Doesn't matter what others think of me.

I am not the source by which I'm sustained.
Have to power,
Own no tower,
I'm just a soul
A mass of flesh,
With reckless propensities
I'm merely a man.

My mind gets cloudy
My soul confused,
My flesh demands
By others feel used.

Doesn't matter how much I see myself to be;
Doesn't matter what others think of me.

Freedom my hearts cry,
Liberty of depleted soul.
Twisted tormented untamed,
So young and yet so old.

Spirit bent on the drug effect of religion surging
through my veins.
Head cocked back
Blaring church music,
Images of cathedrals, church folk and money lines;
Yet so far so far from the real King.

Wearing black,
Feeling blue,
Smiling,
Nodding,
Sideways walking.

Finally exhausted.
Feet bleeding,
Heart beating,
Desperately needing
A remedy.

Reaching past the clouds
Breaking the speed of sound,
Shattering the hardened ground of my heart
God arrives.

Blinds my eyes with the light of His love;
Providential life,
New sight,
I breath afresh,
My soul finds rest.

Joy burst forth,
I am whole.
No longer shattered;
That's all that matters.

....

Enjoy the video
commentary
and reading of
this poem by
William Owens

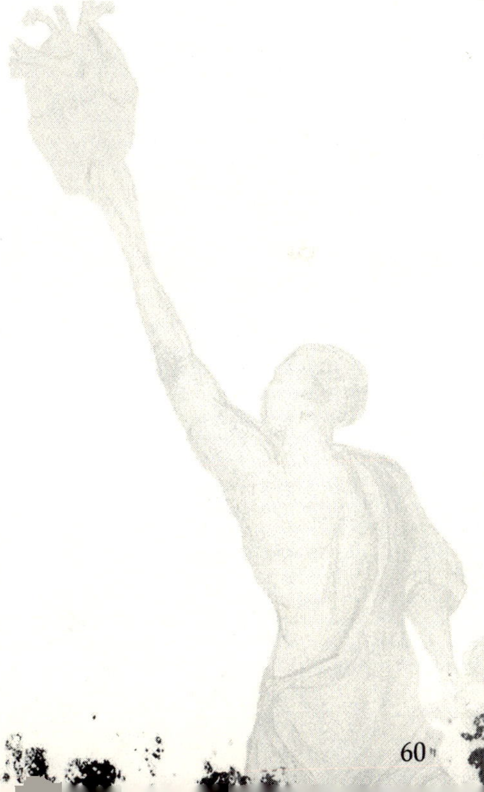

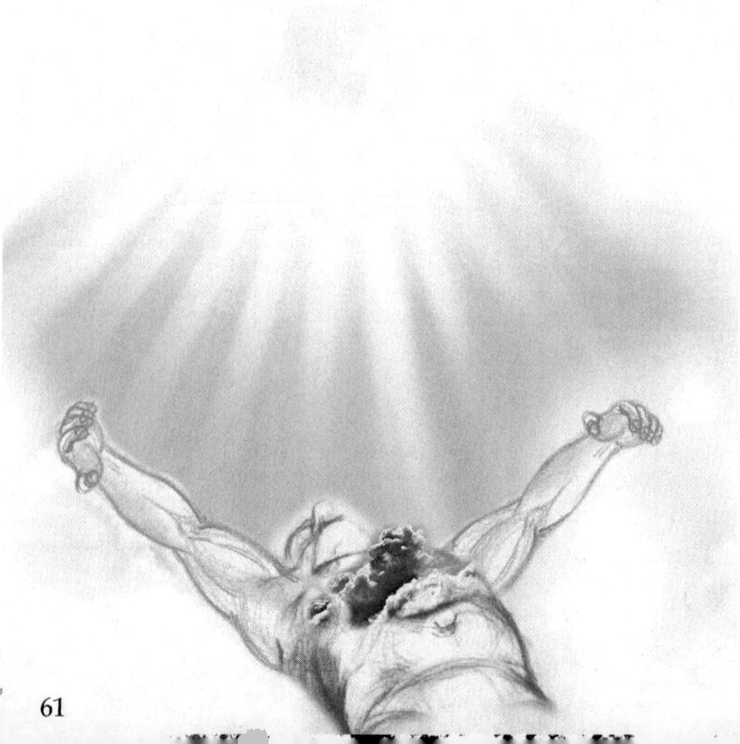

THE DARK LIGHT OF MY SOUL

The Dark Light comes upon me,
To draw me
Near thee.
To force me to see
Things beyond the horizon that I want to believe are true.

Not things, but You;
Not them but me.
Desperate to be
Searching the crevice of my mind, to rectify my life.
I feel damned,
Wanting to be free
Concoctions of my own
tangles my soul.
I be bound,
I be alone.

The Dark Light comes upon me
To draw me near Thee.
To force me to see things beyond the horizon,
that I want to believe are true.

Friends cannot be
What I need.
No fault of theirs,
Faults with me.
I choose in them
What I want to see.
To believe not what I hear,
Instead I dread the fear
Of the Dark Light.

Using the bodies of others
To Shield me from this fight.

I enter this Dark Light alone.
No other can,
No other need,
No other is me,
No other calls me.

I hear His voice
calling my being
Into this place of Darkness.
For what I cannot see is truly true.
What I see has lied to me,
What I see I want to see.

I fight with the inward man
Against the one who loved, loves, and will forever love me.
Shame covers me.
His love forgives,
Embraces,
Washes,
Redeems,
Completes,
Exalts
And Sings!

Finally,
My destiny
Brings me
To the entry
Of the doorway of the Dark Light.
I step forward;
I begin,
I believe,
I see...my Savior.

I am Embraced.

I am changed.
My heart,
My mind,
My will,
Rearranged.

My Dark Light
Made bright.
No fear
Only fight
For right…
Eousness??????

No longer damned,
No longer alone.
New friends I have
Who've tread this path.

I am compelled to usher you
Towards the Dark Light of your soul…

Go,
Be not afraid,
Only believe…

He is waiting.

Enjoy the video commentary and reading of this poem by William Owens

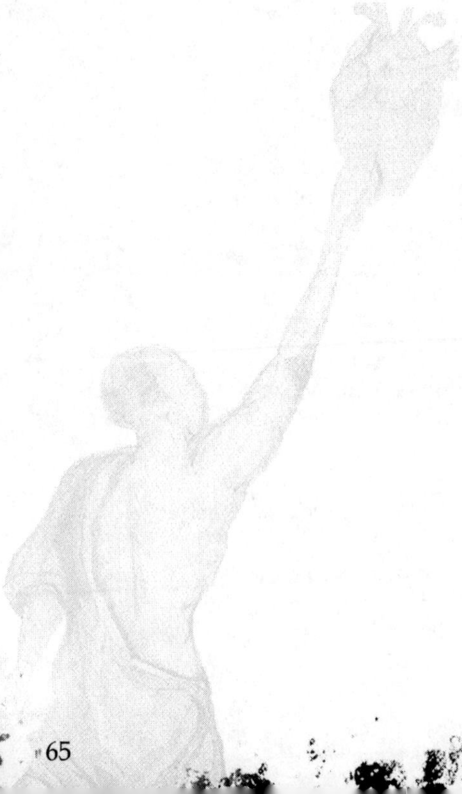

I JUDGE MYSELF NO MORE

I judge myself as if I know
The fabric of my creation.
The logic of my mind,
The depths of my heart,
The intent of my soul.

In arrogance I prance,
In stupidity I dance
On floors of fragmented glass,
Jagged marble toilets.
Forbade sought out comforts
Not to be had.

I judge myself as if I care
Dodging the arrows of blame.
Quenching the fiery flames
With exclusive excuses.
Passive conjectures of reason
Trying to hide my pain.

I judge myself as if I see
Self enduced imagination.
Pictures of stagnation.
Movies on the screen of my brain
Produced by fear, Edited by rejection, Music by neglect.
A victim of myself more than others;
Me and I - a reject,
Others I elect
To tell me who I am.

I judge myself as I feel
Like I can know what's true.

Through touching and seeing,
Even why - through hurt - I'm bleeding.
Ridiculous rationale,
I'm a fools fool thinking others can't tell.

I feel as if it matters,
Lacks power,
No unction.

A mere fabrication of Pride
That doeth ride me silly.
Cascades of folly
Minuscule it makes me.
Deceived deeply,
Drinking in vanity
on Ice.

The Judge has arrived,
Sits high upon His bench.
My sin - a stench,
I'm trapped with this guilt.
Judged to the hilt
Grappling for hope.

Tension rising,
Judge is standing,
Condemning coming,
Escape Improbable,
Forgiveness impossible.

A Whisper in my heart I do hear,
An Advocate next to me - did appear.
Redemption offered
Remove my guilt,
Erase the shame,
Make things new-

Remove the blame.

I ask the price.
With eyes a blaze He shows it all;
The death of Him upon the cross.
Looks at me and says, It's paid in full
Follow me
To be free.
With weary soul
I shudder.
I lose my composure
Collapse a level lower.
His hand grabs my shoulders
I with remaining strength.... repent.

Judge brings gavel down,
Case dismissed is hurled aloud.
Joy runs throughout the crowd of angelic host.
Not seen by eye
I judge myself no more.
For me to live is Christ,
I was judged dead
But Christ has made me alive.

I judge myself no more.
Judge myself no more.
I am free
I have been restored.

....

Enjoy the video commentary and reading of this poem by William Owens

79

ALL THAT MATTERS

Matters not what the day brings;
You made the day.
Matters not if the bird sings;
You write the songs
Matters not what others think,
you know all thoughts.

What matters is my yielded will;
My mind obedient,
My heart surrendered,
My spirit repentive.

My strength devoted,
My soul captured
My being mastered
By you.

Matters not if I breathe,
You are my air.
Matters not if I'm loved by those I see,
You are my love.
You live inside of me.

Matters not if I succeed,
If I win,
If I lose.
If I am honored,
If I'm booed.

You are my life.
You are my joy.

You are my constant friend and my Lord.
You are my everything.
That's all that matters.

SHADES OF LIFE

Shades of life
Flow through our minds;
Seeking, searching, grappling to find
Our destiny before
Our regrets behind.

Shades of life
Demanding of us
To define.
To see the contrast
Of the line,
Of our life.
By the shades
That doeth tell
That in time will reveal
Who we really are.

....

Enjoy the video commentary and reading of this poem by William Owens

73

I SEE THE PAIN

I see the pain
Etched on the arm,
Growing on your face,
Moving in the dance.

It moves you, rolls you,
Never consoles you.
Pushing you, pulling you,
Saying things to you.

Reminding you of you yesterday,
Showing you, you today.
Prophesying of you tomorrow,
The pain is speaking...

Relief you find time to time
Through a fix of some kind.
A drink,
A draw ,
Of maybe that (sniff) white line.

I see the pain
Etched on the arm.
Growing on your face
Moving in the dance.

Your tears testify
Of hope within your grasp.
Too easy you think,
This promise of rest.

Your pain was laid upon Him,
Slayed Him to death - for your death.
Hope burst forth from the Tomb
With power, to assure your rest.
I see your joy
His arm around you,
Face upon you,
You dancing around Him.
I see your pain
No more.

....

Enjoy the video commentary and reading of this poem by William Owens

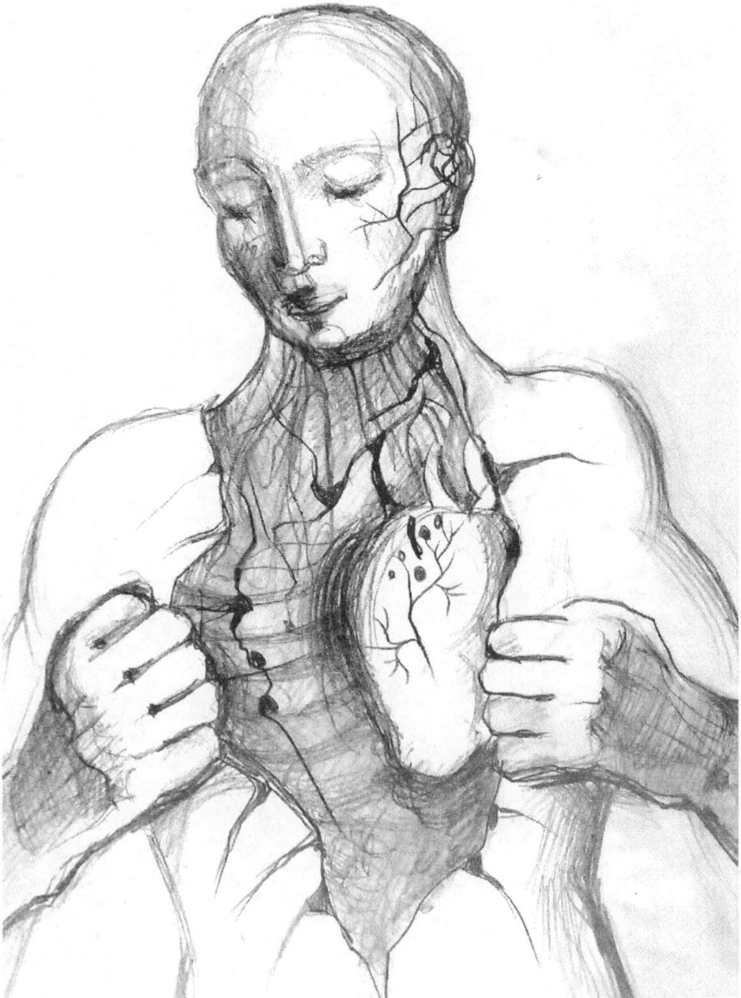

SCARS

Hidden deep within the reservoir of our beings
Traced back to times past.
Shadows.
Alleys.
Thin corridors
That trap us into a vortex of regret,
That grip us with crippling pain around our necks.
Anger.
Resentment.
And...can't think
Again and again and again.
This ride is sick.

What of it?
Who is it?
The scar
I can feel it,
Smell it.
Defiled,
Deformed,
Not how I was born.
How I became
When life came my way.

I dress myself
Put gloss on my face.
Smile to cover the evidence
of my current state.
Limited,
Bound,
Off guard
I do frown.

Push back
Closed up,
Bottled up,
Messed up.
But you can't tell
Because
I'm dressed up.

Gloss on my face
To hide the trace
That leads to the scar
On my heart.

Screaming but can't be heard,
Running but can't be outrun.
Winning but can't win enough,
Losing again what I've already lost before.

Pulling skin like a crazy man,
Ripping veins deep within.
Metaphorically of course,
Actually its worse.

Scars mar,
Rearrange the site.
Misdirect the fight.
Allusions
of the worse outcome
Create fear that makes one run.
Disillusioned,
Confusion,
Rooted in that line upon the heart
That damn scar.

No antidote at the store,
No drink can restore

Money - That's funny!
Most shrinks stink.
Friends?
What's that?

One source alone can
Dissolve,
Remove,
Restore,
Make new.

Go back to that entry way,
Go back until you find the place.
See it,

Feel it,
Grab hold now...
Forgive it,
Forgive them
And live again.
This alone can remove that damning scar.
Within,...
Upon,...
And around
Your heart.

Deeper than the skin that covers us,
Not always drawing blood from us.

Scars upon the heart.

Enjoy the video commentary and reading of this poem by William Owens

WHY?

Why reveals the heartbeat of who we are.
The reason why we do,
The core of our existence.
The passion that drives us,
Compels us,
Infuses us,
Commits us.

Why I ask...you
My eyes looking deep within your soul I want to know why?
Why me?
Why you?
What is it?
What do we do?
Why our paths do cross.
Why our words do intersect.
Connect our minds.
Connect our hearts.

Why? I ask,
Why?

Don't play with me,
Toy with me.
Make light of me.
Fantasy is vanity,
Vanity is insanity.
Insanity is existing not living,
Void of knowing.
The why of you,
The purpose of you,
The core of you.

Tell me WHY?!

Ok,
You don't know.

Then what of me?
How do I fit in your soul?
A soul void of knowing oneself,
Of loving oneself,
Of being oneself.

How can you see me
When your eyes can't see you?
Refuse to be,
Refuse to know.
Who
You
Are.
For you I cry.
Not knowing,
Not living,
Not soaring,
In your why.

I must be.
I must do.
What I know
I see,
I believe,
I am,
Embrace fully my why.
Look into my eye
Don't you see it?

Open your ear
Can't you hear it? I'm living
My why...

Now excuse me.

....

Enjoy the video commentary and reading of this poem by William Owens

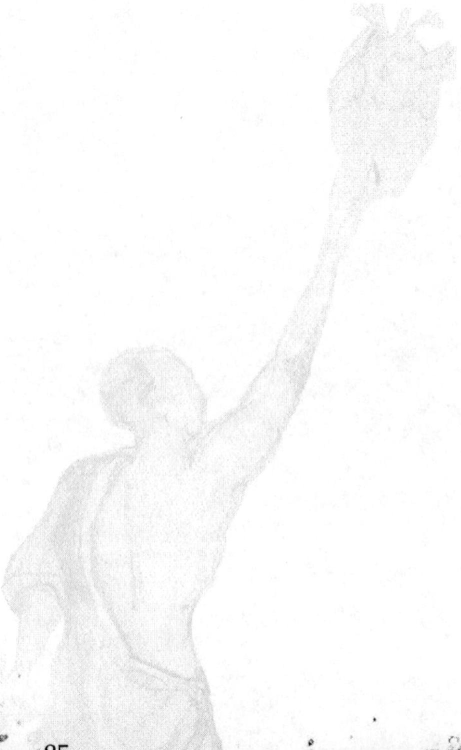

MY MOTHER

He knew me before the earth was formed.
Observed my days
Both first and last.
Placed in me both wit and grit,
Made me a fighter that would never quit...

My days were done,
God had his fun.
In making me,
Shaping me,
Creating in me
Uniqueness,
A godly perspective

He glanced over heavens balcony,
Chose the womb prepared for me.
Got the loins BAM! that was done.

Her womb would carry me ,
Nurture me into the vision
That He did see.

She would shout,
She would dance,
Pray and sing,
Read the word.
Prophesy of things
Not yet seen but believed,
Yes all these things had a part in me.
The me that you see I am no other,
God couldn't have done it like this without my Mother .

Happy Birthday

Enjoy the video commentary and reading of this poem by William Owens

Dangerous Wonders

Dangerous wonder is calling me
Away from my complacency
From the drudgery of doing the nothingness
Of the life that I think I see
That I want - That I feel

A life of mimicking the crowd
Prisoners of a matrix
Illusion created by fear driven anxiety
Maligning and contriving a false narrative about me
To arrest
Destroy
Make void
My destiny

Dangerous wonder is calling me
Into the sphere of the unknown
Yet more real than eye can see
Spiritual realms, angelic host
Vision imparted where faith rules
And children dream and fly
To places unknown to the natural mind
Not seen by eye…. of flesh

I've gotten lost in the shuffle of a life of a lie
Pursuing the goal of living, possessing, eating and dressing
Filled with the temporal, existing outwardly
Inwardly I have died - lost the vision of my childhood
I no longer thrive, press for the prize
I simply master existing - not being alive

Dangerous wonder is calling me
No loud voice demanding my attention
Threatening for my affection
Twisting my brain with insane images of condemnation
It be a soft voice deep within my true self
Reminding me of dreams, visions and careless abandonment
To a higher place of purpose, a fearlessness

Carefree glee, cape on my back
I'm going to fly . . . High

Taking rides in realms unseen by mortal eye
More real than country tis of thee
Beyond the zip code where I do live
This chain, this trap, this lie

The grip of society on my brain, taking me prisoner with chain
Creating pain within my soul - has stolen my why
I am lost and know it not
Successful at what?
Possessed by possessions - no longer dreaming
Just leaning on props made of wood, stubble and hay
All soon to whither away
Being blown by the winds of change
Less we embrace the dangerous wonder
Given by God who is our truest friend

A journey beyond the pale, stale temporal sphere
Into a world beyond the gaze of eye
Only seen by children at heart
Running through fields of dreams
laughing with joy unfeigned
Daringly embracing the call - rising above it all
To fly high - past the sky - with cape on tight
In childlike faith - taking up the fight
Of dangerous wonder

No shame No fear
No regret or retreat
Only magnificent delight
As I answer God's call that has called me
That is calling me - that will call me throughout my life.
In and through His Son
Jesus the Risen Christ!

Enjoy the video commentary and reading of this poem by William Owens

SLANDERED

Has anyone slandered you openly before the world?
Hurled insults, called you names to inflict pain upon your heart?
Created thoughts within your brain that cause emotional strain?

Someone who thought they knew
Understood the facts,
Calling blue pink and green black.
No resolve to seek healing
To follow Christ's example,
Instead they attack.

When it happens,
(and it will)
Don't snap back.
Pray.
Stay calm.
Ask God for understanding,
As to what to do.
Sometimes it's just the enemy trying to provoke you.

Seek solutions,
Engage with intent.
To seek healing
If necessary, repent.

Whatever you do
Don't stoop,
Stand tall.
Be resolved.
Be the vessel of grace, of love and of patience,
That God would use to bring the hope and power of
Reconciliation.

Enjoy the video commentary and reading of this poem by William Owens

THE ENEMY WANTS YOU TO SEE

The enemy wants you to see what's not there,
What's not true,
What's a lie,
Even what others see of you.

Doesn't want you to see the truth
Of who are are.
The truth of God's eye upon you,
His thoughts towards you,
His vision for you.

The enemy is never far
Whispers ideas,
Presses upon your ears.
Relentless,
Senseless,
Rude,
Crude,
Vile
Detestable
Lies.

Scars upon your mind
He wants to inflict.
To paralyze your commitment.
To ostracize your connection.
To pervert your reflection.
To minimize your perception.
To void your destiny.

The eye of the Almighty,
Gentle grace
Doeth embrace.
Shine upon your face
rays of hope,
vision within.
Dispels the enemies lies without.

Tell him,
Declare to him,
Challenge and confront Him.
It will be the end of him.

....

Enjoy the video
commentary
and reading of
this poem by
William Owens

I AM A SPIRIT

I am a Spirit,
Not the flesh you do see.
I am a Spirit,
Made to live throughout eternity.
A spirit who knows more than what these eyes see.
A spirit housed in clay
Created to be free.

I live in a realm unseen by most
I pursue a purpose.
Beyond the coast of the common, the mundane.
The deceptive desires of mere man.

I am a spirit made in the image of my Beloved.
Whose sonship was confirmed by God's voice and a dove.

A spirit known before the space called time,
To thrive not exist .
To conquer, not be conquered.
To do all things,
Not a few things.
To love,
To walk on water,
To achieve what I believe.

I'm a spirit
Fierce for truth.
Abounding in grace,
Honestly contending for my faith.
Though not perfect
Yet made perfect,
I exist in this tension.

No longer a prisoner
A spirit warrior,
A contender for the prize
I shall arise a winner...

I am a spirit,
Not the flesh you do see.

....

Enjoy the video commentary and reading of this poem by William Owens

SPIRITUAL RHYTHM

Spiritual,
Not temporary
The real realm of reality.
The motion of devotion
Doeth leap from heart broken.

The struggle,
The failure
When I yield to my pleasure.

Senseless
Relentless
Ignorant of the consequences
When I fail to repent.

To realign with Life ,
To regain my rhythm
Of the spiritual
Of the real.

Day by day,
Moment by moment
Must I stay synced with the Spirit's motion.

Humble,
Contrite,
Broken,
Yielded;
Fearful of prides poison
My rebellious mind notions.

Spiritual
Not temporary,
The real realm of reality.
The motion of devotion
Doeth leap from heart broken.
The joy
The bliss,
As I stay in His rest.
As I flow,
As I breathe ,
To be
To live.

Liberated
Through
His
Rhythm.
Arranged... for me.

By faith I do step into this ordained Symphony...

of Love.
By His Spirit...
In His rhythm...

Enjoy the video commentary and reading of this poem by William Owens

HEART CORDS

Heart cords run deep,
Attached to every sector of my life.
Registers my joys, pains, miseries and strife.

Bumps on the screen
Doeth scream
Of cords taking in
The pulse of my life, my day, my reasons for being.

Heart cords
Tangled with others.
Mangled with incisions,
Made numb by indecision,
Yet alive by a deep embedded vision.

Reaching, stretching, seeking for that connection.
Heart cords longing for the home
From which they've come.
The home to which they belong.

My heart cords plugged in
To Him alone.
Made bright,
Given rest,
Connected,
Respected.
No more to be rejected.
Restored,
Made whole,
Heart cords turned gold.

Enjoy the video commentary and reading of this poem by William Owens

THE TRUTH DOES NOT SCARE

The truth does not scare.
Will never be moved
By voices, images, the spirit of fear.
Or that false sense of despair.

The truth,
No abstract idea
Concoctions of man
Well thought-out plan.
Scraps of lies,
Smell of flies
Like something died.

The truth,
Bold to the bone.
Towering above all creation.
Without permission
Stands alone.

Makes free
With no key.
Makes alive,
Fire in eye.;

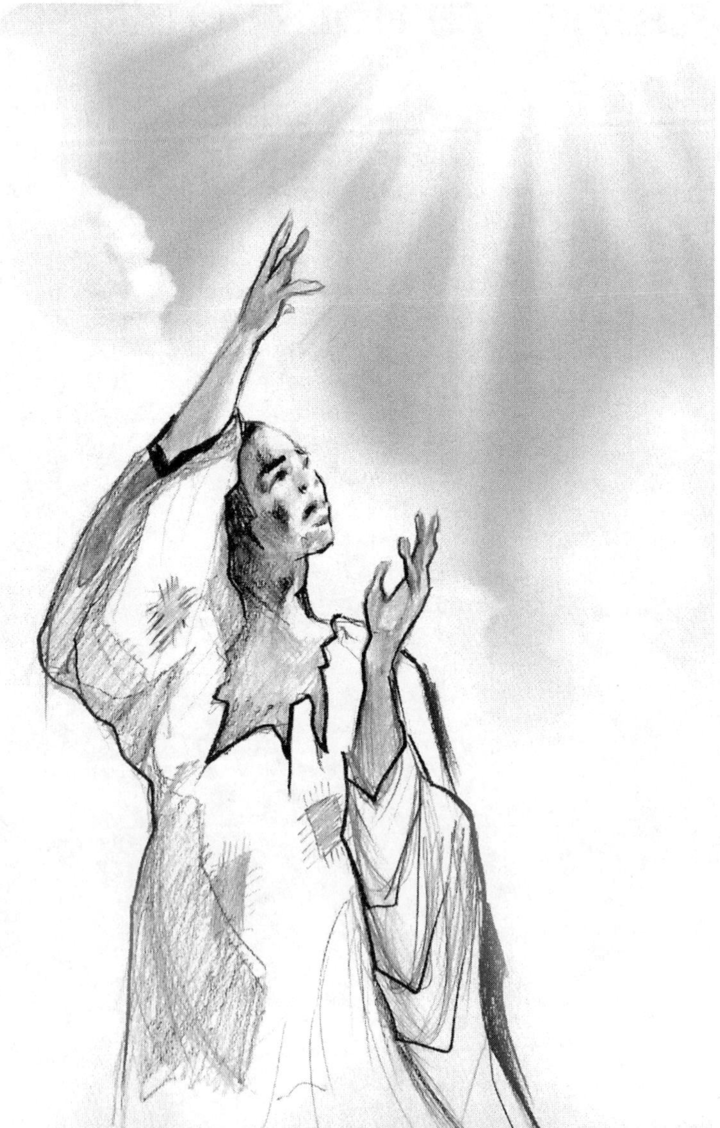

TO LIVE IS TO FORGIVE

For me to live is to forgive.
For me to rise
to thrive,
to be the person God made me
My heart must be ever so free
Of fault toward others,
No matter what they've done or do to me.

The life I live must express more than eye can see.
Hands can feel,
Ears can hear,
Nose can smell,
Heart can tell.

The traps are set,
The bait reflects,
The scent attracts.
Pulls,
Lures,
Feeding on my wounded heart.
My Clouded mind,
My stubborn will,
Refuse to see the truth
I remain blind.

Blind to a healing place
A new beginning.
A freedom from the gnawing pain of slaps against my face.
Of rejections of my soul ,
Of denial of my existence,
Because of my uniqueness.
My smile

My gift
My voice,
And even my race.

It's time to stop,
Exit this trap.

Get off this ride,
Give it no slack.
As I dare to hope and dream
It grabs my neck,
And yanks me back.

I ponder back and forth.
Seeking for a door,
A hole in the floor.
A crack in the wall,
A window to escape the pain.
A prisoner possessed with possessions
But not sane.
Who,
What
How can I breath?
How can I Live?
....I must forgive.

Enjoy the video
commentary
and reading of
this poem by
William Owens

I TURN

I turn and press into your righteousness,
Lest I turn away from your face.

I burn for your holiness,
Less I grow cold towards your love.

I submit to your Lordship,
Less I resist your purpose.

I am nothing without you.
By nature I doubt you,
By faith I take hold of you,
By works I obey.

Servant I am,
Savior you are.
Friend you call me,
Abba I call you.
We are one.

Visit
NakedbeforeGod.com
For updates, blogs and new poems by
William Owens

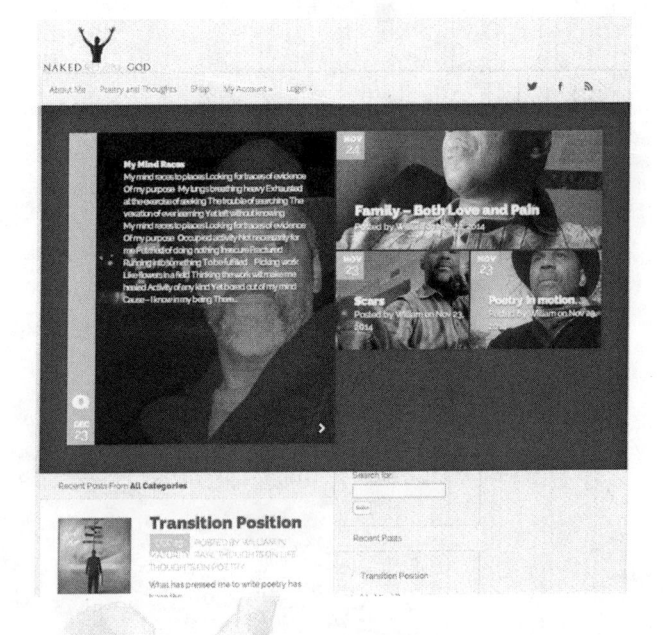